NEW HAVEN FREE PUBLIC LIBRARY

3 5000 08563 9424

DATE DUE

OCT 0 2 2001	MAR 11 2008	
		MAR 0 3 2012 MAY 0 3 2012
IIII 1 5 2003		
NOV 2 0 2003		JUL 3 0 2012
OCT 2 7 2004	APR 2 8 2007	MAR 0 8 2013
APR 1 6 2005	JUN 0 7 2006	NOV 1 6 2013
	MAR 0 6 2010	FEB 1 8 2014
NOV 2 8 2005	MAR 0 6 2010	AUG 3 0 2014
		DEC 1 7 2016
	FEB 0 5 2011	
APR 0 7 2007		
AUG 1 8 2007	MAR 1 9 2011	
	JUN 1 8 2011	
OCT 1 6 2009	DEC 3 0 2011	

The SUN

Robin Kerrod

Lerner Publications Company • Minneapolis

This edition published in 2000

Lerner Publications Company
A Division of Lerner Publishing Group
241 First Avenue North, Minneapolis MN 55401

Website address: www.lernerbooks.com

© 2000 by Graham Beehag Books

All U.S. rights reserved. International copyright secured. No
part of this book may be reproduced, stored in a retrieval
system, or transmitted in any form or by any means—
electronic, mechanical, photocopying, recording, or
otherwise—without the prior written permission of
Lerner Publications Company, except for the inclusion of
brief quotations in an acknowledged review.

Library of Congress Cataloging-in-Publication Data

Kerrod, Robin
    The Sun / Robin Kerrod.
       p. cm. – (Planet library)
    Includes index.
    Summary: Introduces the Sun, our star, its relationship to
 other stars, its solar system, and the effects it has on Earth.
    ISBN 0-8225-3901-2 (lib.. bdg.)
    1. Sun—Juvenile literature. 2. astronomy—
 Juvenile literature. [1. Sun.]
    I. Title. II Series: Kerrod, Robin. Planet library.
    QB521.5.K47 2000   98-54438
    523.7—dc21

Printed in Singapore by Tat Wei Printing Packaging Pte Ltd
Bound in the United States of America
1 2 3 4 5 6 – OS – 05 04 03 02 01 00

CHILDREN'S ROOM

j523.7
KERROD

CONTENTS

Target Schools
Public Library
Partnership Fund

WARNING!

Never look directly at the Sun. In particular, never look at the Sun through binoculars or a telescope. If you do, you will damage your eyes and may go blind.

A streamer of glowing gas thousands of miles long shoots high above the Sun's surface. In time, the gas will cool and fall back into the Sun.

Introducing the Sun

To us on Earth, the Sun is by far the most important body in the heavens. It sends us light to see by and heat to keep us warm. Without the Sun's light and heat, plants could not grow. Then there would be no food for other living things. Earth would be a dark, cold, and dead world.

The Sun and Earth travel together through space. Earth is one of many bodies that circle around the Sun. Together, these bodies form the Sun's family, the solar system. The word *solar* comes from the Latin word for the Sun, *Sol*.

The Sun is the only body in the solar system that gives off its own light. Planets and moons only reflect light from the Sun. The Sun is a star. It looks bigger and brighter than the other stars in the night sky because it is much closer.

Like the other stars, the Sun is a huge ball of extremely hot glowing gas. Its glaring surface is stormy and always changing. Great fiery fountains suddenly spring up. Dark spots come and go. Streams of particles flow out into space like a wind, causing spectacular effects when they reach Earth.

Astronomers think that the Sun is 4.6 billion years old. They believe it will probably keep on shining as it does for another 5 billion years. Then it will start to die. In time it will fade and shrink to a dark ball of cinders not much bigger than Earth.

Symbol for the Sun

The Sun God

Ancient peoples knew how important the Sun was to them, and they worshiped it as a god. In ancient Egypt, for example, Re was worshiped as the Sun god and the creator of all things.

The Sun sinks below the western horizon at sunset. The sky turns red because the dusty atmosphere reflects red light from the Sun better than light of other colors.

Our Star, the Sun

The Sun is quite unlike any other body in the solar system because it is a star. It makes its own energy and pours this energy into space as light and heat. But it is a very ordinary kind of star.

Like all stars, the Sun is a great ball of very hot gases. The main gas is called hydrogen. We know that the Sun is very hot because we can feel its heat a long way away, on Earth. Earth lies about 93 million miles (nearly 150 million km) away from the Sun.

In our skies, the Sun looks much bigger and very much brighter than the other stars. But as stars go, the Sun is not very big or very bright. It only seems bigger and brighter to us because it is much nearer. The nearest stars are not just millions of miles away, they are millions of millions of miles away. Imagine that our Sun was the size of a grain of sand and located in New York City. On the same scale, the nearest star would be another grain of sand located in San Francisco.

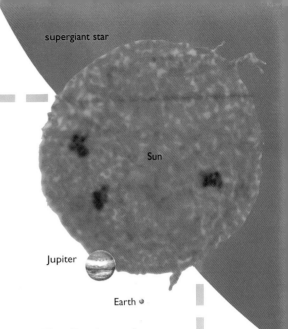

Sun

Jupiter

Earth

The Sun measures about 865,000 miles (1,400,000 km) in diameter. That is more than a hundred times bigger than Earth. But for a star, the Sun is actually small. Astronomers classify the Sun as a dwarf star. They call it a yellow dwarf because the light it gives out is yellowish.

Astronomers can figure out the temperature of a star from the color of the light it gives out. They have found that the temperature on the surface of the Sun is about 10,000° F (5,500° C).

INSIDE THE SUN

Inside, the Sun is much hotter. In the core, or center, the temperature is estimated to rise as high as 27,000,000° F (15,000,000° C). This great heat affects the hydrogen in the core. It brings about nuclear fusion.

In nuclear fusion, the atoms, or smallest particles, of hydrogen fuse, or join together. They form another gas called helium. When this happens, enormous amounts of energy are given out. This energy gradually makes its way up to the surface of the Sun. There it is given off into space, mainly as heat and light. Only about $1/2,000,000,000$ of the Sun's heat and light reach Earth—the rest goes into space.

Above: The Sun is much bigger than Earth and even the biggest planet, Jupiter. But it is tiny compared with the biggest stars, which are called supergiants. Some supergiants are 250 million miles (400 million km) across.

Below: Inside the Sun, atoms of hydrogen join together to form helium atoms. This fusion process produces the energy that makes the Sun shine.

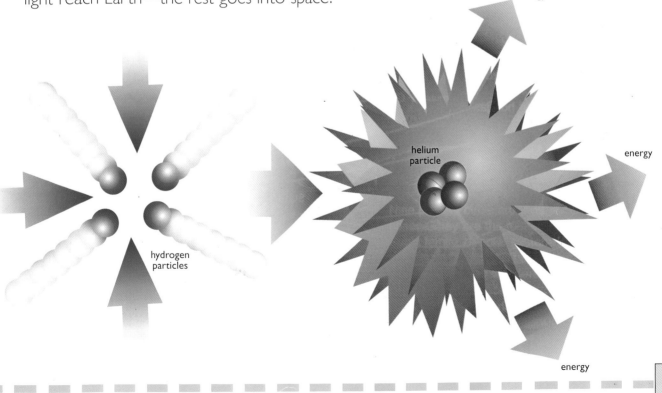

energy

helium particle

energy

hydrogen particles

energy

Surface and Atmosphere

The bright surface of the Sun boils and bubbles as hot gas rises. Jets of fiery gas shoot up hundreds of thousands of miles into the Sun's atmosphere.

The part of the Sun we see is called the photosphere, which means "light ball." It forms a thin shell around the Sun, about 300 miles (500 km) thick. Most of the heat and light the Sun gives out comes from the photosphere.

The photosphere is constantly heaving like a stormy sea as pockets of hot gas bubble up to the surface. These bubbles make the surface look speckled.

SPOTS ON THE SUN

From time to time, dark patches appear on the photosphere. They are called sunspots. They may grow to be much bigger than Earth and may last for months at a time. Sunspots look darker than the rest of the Sun's surface because they are cooler.

Above: The surface of the Sun, pictured by the space probe *SOHO*. The small, bright specks all over the surface show where masses of hot, glowing gas reach the surface. The three large bright patches are powerful solar flares.

Right: A group of sunspots on the Sun's surface. They are about 1,800° F (1,000° C) cooler than the rest of the Sun's surface.

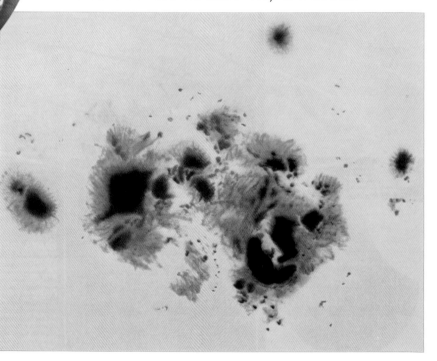

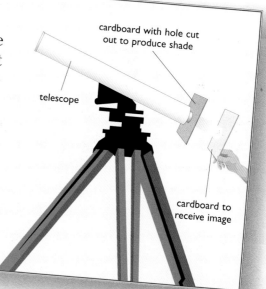

Seeing Sunspots

Using a telescope, you can see sunspots from Earth. But you must not look directly at the Sun because this can seriously damage your eyes. Instead, use the telescope to project an image of the Sun onto a piece of white cardboard. (See diagram at right.) If you watch sunspots from day to day, you will notice that they move across the Sun's surface.

cardboard with hole cut out to produce shade

telescope

cardboard to receive image

A solar flare erupts. A huge sheet of flaming gas springs up in the Sun's lower atmosphere, and streams of particles flow out into space.

Astronomers do not know exactly why sunspots appear. But they do know that it has something to do with the Sun's magnetism, or electrical currents moving across the Sun. The Sun's magnetism is very strong where sunspots appear.

From Earth, we can see the sunspots move from day to day. This is because the Sun is spinning around in space. It takes about 25 Earth-days for the Sun to rotate once.

Sunspots come and go on the Sun's surface. In some years, hardly any sunspots appear. In other years, spots spring up all over the place. On average, a year when the Sun has the most sunspots happens every 11 years. Many sunspots were seen in the year 1990.

THE COLOR BALL

Like Earth, the Sun has an atmosphere made up of layers of gases. The part of the atmosphere just outside the photosphere is called the chromosphere, which means "color ball." It gets this name because it has a pinkish color. It is about 6,000 miles (10,000 km) thick.

Like the photosphere, the chromosphere is in constant motion. Little jets of glowing gas dance all over it all of the time. Sometimes huge flickering tongues spring up, like flames in a fire. They are called solar flares.

A solar flare usually lasts for only a few minutes. But during this time, it may become the brightest feature on the Sun. It gives off enormous amounts of energy, and it sends streams of electric particles out into space.

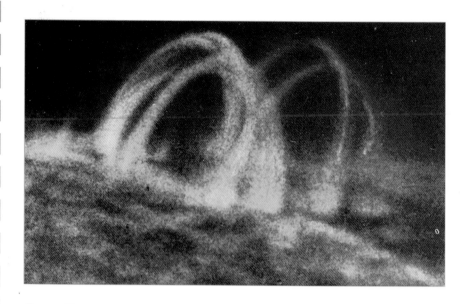

Left: These arches of flaming gas rising high above the Sun are called loop prominences. They form loops when the gas follows the pattern of the Sun's magnetism.

FIERY FOUNTAINS

From time to time, the chromosphere also throws out other jets of flaming gas. They often rise up hundreds of thousands of miles before arching over and plunging back again, somewhat like the water in a fountain. These fiery fountains are called prominences. Prominences often happen close to sunspots. So they are also probably caused by the Sun's magnetism.

THE SUN'S CROWN

Above the chromosphere is the outer layer of the Sun's atmosphere. It is called the corona, which means "crown." It reaches out for millions of miles into space, getting fainter and fainter the farther out it goes.

SEEING THE ATMOSPHERE

The chromosphere and the corona both give off light. But we usually cannot see them because the Sun's surface is so bright. The only time we can see them from Earth is during a total eclipse of the Sun.

Right: This picture from the space probe *SOHO* shows the bright corona stretching out on each side of the Sun. The face of the Sun has been blotted out (center) so that the corona becomes visible. In the background are stars of the constellation Sagittarius. At the bottom, part of the Milky Way galaxy can be seen.

Polar Lights

Auroras take place mainly in the far northern and far southern regions of the world, near the North and South Poles. In the north, they are called the aurora borealis, or the Northern Lights. In the south, they are called the aurora australis, or the Southern Lights. Auroras can take many forms. At their most beautiful, they look like shimmering curtains of colored light.

During a total eclipse, the Moon is positioned between Earth and the Sun and blots out the Sun's light. We can see the chromosphere as a pinkish glow around the edge of the Moon. We can also see prominences, looping up through the chromosphere. Farther out, the corona appears as a pearly white halo.

THE SOLAR WIND

The Sun gives off heat, light, and other rays. It also gives off streams of tiny particles. These particles carry a tiny amount of electricity. They flow out into space in all directions. This flow of particles is called the solar wind.

Usually, the solar wind "blows" gently, like a summer breeze on Earth. But when a flare springs up on the Sun's surface and gives out its great blasts of particles, the solar wind can become a gale.

These particles affect us when they reach Earth. Because they are electric, they can upset our electricity supplies. They can cause interference on the radio. But they also cause beautiful dancing light displays in the sky. These displays are called auroras.

The Sun in the Sky

Every day, the Sun appears to move across the sky, traveling from east to west. As the year goes by, the Sun's path through the sky changes, bringing about regular changes in the weather.

Early every morning on Earth, the Sun rises above the horizon in the east. The sky becomes light, and day begins. During the morning, the Sun climbs higher and higher into the sky, traveling toward the west. It reaches its highest point in the sky at midday, or noon.

In the afternoon, the Sun gradually sinks lower and lower in the sky, still traveling westward. In the evening, it sets below the horizon in the west. When the Sun sets, the sky darkens and night begins. The next morning, the Sun rises in the east again, and daylight returns.

The regular rising and setting of the Sun is one of the basic rhythms of nature. It gives us one of our main units of time, the day.

Opposite: Because Earth spins around in space, the Sun seems to travel across the sky during the day. It rises in the east, reaches its highest point at noon, then sinks below the horizon in the west at sunset.

Shadow Clocks and Sundials

When the Sun shines, objects on the ground cast shadows. The shadows move hour by hour as Earth rotates and the Sun's position in the sky changes. Early peoples used the changing positions of shadows to tell the time. The ancient Egyptians used simple shadow clocks. More elaborate sundials were the main means of telling the time of day until the invention of mechanical clocks in the 1300s.

Sun

THE SPINNING EARTH

Of course, the Sun only looks as if it circles around the Earth in space. In ancient times, people believed it did. But we've learned that in fact it is Earth that is moving, not the Sun.

Earth spins around in space like a top, taking one day to rotate once. It spins around from west to east. This is what makes the Sun seem to travel across the sky in the opposite direction, from east to west.

CIRCLING THE SUN

Earth moves in space in another way. Like all the other planets, it travels in an orbit, or path, around the Sun. It takes Earth a little over 365 days to orbit the Sun once. This period of time is called a year.

The year and the day are our two main natural divisions of time. We use them in our calendars. Calendars are a way of dividing up the year so that people all over the world use the same date at the same time.

Months and weeks are the other divisions of time we use in our calendars. A month is about the time it takes the Moon to circle around Earth. But a week of 7 days does not match up with any natural division of time.

day

night

orbit of Earth

Earth spins around, taking a day to rotate once as it travels in its orbit around the Sun, which takes one year. At any time, half of Earth is in sunlight, and it is daytime. The other half is in shadow, and it is nighttime.

America's Stonehenge, near North Salem, New Hampshire. Large stones were lined up in about 1500 B.C. to mark the positions of sunrise during different seasons.

LEAP YEARS

To be more accurate, it takes Earth 365¼ days to circle once around the Sun. Usually, the year on our calendar is 365 days long. This means that every 4 years, our calendar gets 1 day (4 × ¼ = 1) out of step with the true year according to the Sun.

So every 4 years, an extra day is added to the calendar year, making it 366 days long. This year is called a leap year. The extra day is always added to the month of February, making it 29 instead of 28 days long. Years that you can divide by 4 are leap years. The years 1996 and 2000 were leap years.

EARTH'S TILT

Earth spins around in space. It spins around on an imaginary line called its axis. The line goes through the North and South Poles.

Earth does not spin in an upright position as it circles around the Sun. Its axis is tilted at an angle to the direction in which it is traveling. This means that the northern half of Earth is tilted toward the Sun for half of the year and away from the Sun for the other half. When the northern half of Earth is tilted toward the Sun, it receives more of the Sun's heat and the weather is warmer. When it is tilted away from the Sun, it receives less heat and the weather is colder.

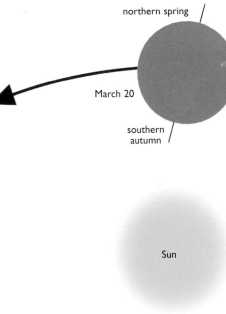

northern spring

March 20

southern autumn

northern summer

June 21

southern winter

Sun

northern autumn

September 22

southern spring

The Midnight Sun

Fort Yukon, Alaska, lies on the Arctic Circle. Every year on June 21 the Sun is still shining at midnight at Fort Yukon. On that date, the Sun does not set, and there is daylight all night long. The midnight Sun also shines on that date at every other place in the world on the Arctic Circle. At places farther north, people can see the midnight Sun for longer periods of time. In parts of northern Norway, people can see the midnight Sun for up to three months, from May to July. That is why the country is called the "land of the midnight Sun."

THE FOUR SEASONS

The changes in temperature caused by Earth's tilt take place regularly every year. They help us divide the year into periods called the seasons. In many parts of the world, there are four seasons: spring, summer, autumn, and winter.

Winter is the time when a place is tilted away from the Sun and the weather is cold. The Sun travels lower in the sky, days are shorter, and nights are longer. Summer is the time when a place is tilted toward the Sun and the weather is warm. The Sun travels higher in the sky, days are longer, and nights are shorter. Spring is the time between winter and summer when the weather is warming up. Autumn is the time between summer and winter when the weather is cooling down.

In North America and other places in the Northern Hemisphere, spring starts on about March 20, summer on about June 21, autumn on about September 22, and winter on about December 21.

In Australia and other places in the Southern Hemisphere, the seasons are reversed. For example, winter happens there when the Northern Hemisphere has summer. This is because when the Northern Hemisphere tilts most toward the Sun, the Southern Hemisphere tilts most away from the Sun.

northern winter

December 21

southern summer

In the Shadows

Sometimes the Moon passes in front of the Sun in the sky and blocks out its light. For a while, day becomes night. The air cools, and birds, thinking it is evening, start to roost.

Earth travels through space with a companion, the Moon. The Moon circles around Earth, while Earth circles around the Sun. With the Sun's light shining on Earth and the Moon, they both make shadows in space, just as you make shadows on the ground when you stand in sunlight.

Sun

Moon

partial shadow
(penumbra)

complete shadow
(umbra)

Earth

In July 1991, one of the longest total eclipses of the century took place in Hawaii. Here we see the Moon covering two-thirds of the Sun. It is midmorning, but light is fading fast.

A few times every year, the Sun, the Moon, and Earth line up exactly, or almost exactly, in space. When the Moon comes between the Sun and Earth, it makes a shadow that falls on Earth. Someone in the shadow would see the Moon cover all or part of the Sun. This is called an eclipse of the Sun, or a solar eclipse. When the Moon covers all of the Sun, it is called a total eclipse. When the Moon covers only part of the Sun, it is called a partial eclipse.

At other times when the Sun, Earth, and the Moon are lined up, Earth's shadow falls on the Moon. This is called an eclipse of the Moon, or a lunar eclipse. The Moon does not completely disappear from view during a lunar eclipse. It is still lit up by faint light coming around Earth and usually looks red.

WARNING!

You need to look through a special filter to see an eclipse of the Sun. Do not use a piece of over-exposed photographic film or a piece of smoked glass. These will block out the Sun's glare but might let invisible rays through that could damage your eyes.

TOTAL ECLIPSE

During a solar eclipse, the Moon's shadow covers only a small area of Earth's surface. Only people within that area will see a total eclipse. And they see it only for a short period of time. This is because the shadow races across Earth as Earth rotates and the Moon moves overhead.

Total eclipses are among the great spectacles of nature. During a total eclipse, astronomers can study the Sun's atmosphere. They can see the fiery fountains called prominences and the white corona. Astronomers travel all over the world to see and photograph total eclipses.

STAR POINT

The longest a total eclipse of the Sun can last is about 7½ minutes. But most eclipses are much shorter.

The July 1991 total eclipse in Hawaii. Totality, the period of darkness, lasted for more than four minutes. During this time, the Sun's corona shone around the dark Moon. The sky did not go totally dark; it became orange on the horizon, like it often does at sunset.

Frightening the Dragon

Eclipses of the Sun terrified ancient peoples because they did not know what was happening. They thought that some great heavenly monster was trying to swallow the Sun. They knew that if it succeeded they would be doomed, because the Sun brings life to Earth. The ancient Chinese pictured the monster as a dragon. When they saw it starting to swallow the Sun, they banged gongs and cymbals and made as much noise as they could to frighten it away. They found this always worked.

The Life-Giving Sun

The Sun pours out fantastic amounts of heat and light into space. Only a small fraction of this energy reaches Earth. But it is enough to breathe life into our planet.

Redwoods, growing in northern California. They are among the tallest living things on Earth, sometimes growing to a height of more than 300 feet (90 m).

There are millions of different species, or kinds, of living things on Earth. Some, like bacteria, are so small that you can see them only under a microscope. Others, like sequoia trees and blue whales, are truly gigantic.

Large or small, plants and animals can stay alive only under certain conditions. For one thing, they must live at a temperature that is not too hot and not too cold.

The Sun provides Earth with just the right amount of heat to keep it at a comfortable temperature for life. Earth is just the right distance away from the Sun for this to happen. If it were much closer to the Sun, it would get too hot for life. If it were much farther away, it would get too cold.

A deer drinks water in a stream. It is one of hundreds of thousands of different animal species that live on Earth. Like all animals, it cannot make its own food. It has to eat plants, which can make their own food.

Gas burns on an offshore oil rig, releasing the energy of "stored sunlight." Oil is the remains of tiny plants that, millions of years ago, grew by trapping the energy in sunlight.

FOOD FOR LIFE

Another essential thing plants and animals must have to stay alive is food. Food provides the energy to grow and to stay alive. Only plants can make their own food. Animals have to eat plants or eat animals that eat plants.

A plant makes its food from water and carbon dioxide gas. In a plant's green leaves, water and carbon dioxide combine to form a simple sugar. This is the plant's food. But the process can only take place in sunlight. The energy in sunlight is needed to make the water and carbon dioxide combine. The process is called photosynthesis, which means "making with light."

Sugar, the food the plant makes, is full of energy. We can think of sugar as "stored sunlight" because the plant has made it by using, or trapping, the energy in sunlight. When animals eat plants as food, they are in fact feeding on stored sunlight.

Stored sunlight also provides most of the energy the world uses. Coal, oil, and natural gas are all forms of stored sunlight. Coal is made up of the remains of giant ferns and other plants that once grew on Earth. Oil and natural gas are made up of the remains of tiny plants that lived in ancient seas. When we burn these fuels, we release energy that plants trapped from the Sun hundreds of millions of years ago.

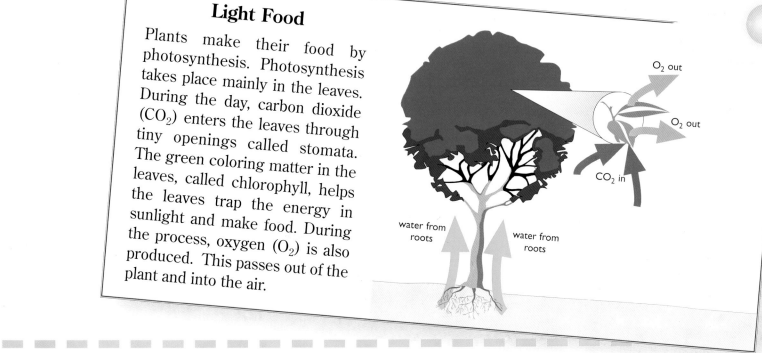

Light Food

Plants make their food by photosynthesis. Photosynthesis takes place mainly in the leaves. During the day, carbon dioxide (CO_2) enters the leaves through tiny openings called stomata. The green coloring matter in the leaves, called chlorophyll, helps the leaves trap the energy in sunlight and make food. During the process, oxygen (O_2) is also produced. This passes out of the plant and into the air.

O_2 out

O_2 out

CO_2 in

water from roots

water from roots

A rainbow is one of the most beautiful sights in nature. You see a rainbow in the sky when the Sun is shining in the sky behind you and it is raining in front of you. The rainbow is red on the outside and violet inside. Sometimes you can see a double rainbow. The fainter rainbow has the colors reversed, with red on the inside and violet on the outside.

A yellow flower looks yellow because it reflects only yellow light. Leaves look green because they reflect only green light.

white
sunlight

Coloring the World

The light that comes from the Sun looks white, but it is actually made up of many colors. When the Sun shines through raindrops, we see these colors in the sky as a rainbow.

We see seven main colors in a rainbow: violet, indigo, blue, green, yellow, orange, and red. But what do these colors mean? To find out, we must first look at the nature of light itself. Light is a kind of energy that travels in the form of waves, like the ripples on a pond. We can picture it like this:

The distance between the top of one wave and the top of the next is called the wavelength. Light of a certain color has a certain wavelength. So each color in the rainbow is made up of light of a unique wavelength.

The Sun gives out light of all these wavelengths, which appear as colors. When these colors are mixed together, they make white light—the light we usually see. This light splits into its different colors to form a rainbow when it passes through raindrops.

We can produce an artificial rainbow by passing light through a wedge of glass, or prism. The prism splits up the light into its different wavelengths. It produces a spread of colors called a spectrum.

COLOR REFLECTIONS

Of course, we see color all around us, not only in the sky. What gives objects their color? We can explain this since we know that light is made up of many colors.

We see objects because they reflect light into our eyes. When they reflect all the white light that falls on them, we see them as white. But objects absorb, or take in, some of the colors from the light that falls on them. We see them in the colors they reflect. For example, the flower of a dandelion absorbs all the colors in light except for yellow. It reflects the yellow light into our eyes.

We can split white light into its different colors by passing it through a prism. As the light passes through the prism, it bends. But each color bends a different amount. Red light bends the least, violet light the most. In this way, the different colors fan out to form a spectrum.

Invisible Rays

Light is one form in which the Sun gives off energy. We can see the light rays with our eyes. The Sun also gives off heat. We can feel the heat rays with our skin, but we cannot see them. They are invisible. The Sun also gives off many other kinds of invisible rays. They include X rays, ultraviolet rays, infrared rays, and radio waves.

Some of these rays would be dangerous to us if they reached the ground. But most of them are blocked by Earth's atmosphere. Only some ultraviolet rays come through. These are the rays that burn your skin if you stay out in the Sun too long.

The Sun and the Universe

For us, the Sun is the most important heavenly body there is. But in the Universe as a whole, it is not very important at all. There are billions upon billions of stars like it.

1. A massive explosion takes place on the Sun.

The Universe includes everything that exists. Long ago, people believed that Earth was the center of the Universe. They thought that the Sun, the planets, and the stars circled around the Earth.

In the 1500s, astronomers realized that Earth was a planet that circled around the Sun. Then they thought that the Sun was the center of the Universe.

By the beginning of the 20th century, astronomers knew that the Sun was just one of billions of stars in a star system they called the Galaxy. And they thought that the Galaxy was the entire Universe.

2. Some of the millions of stars that travel through space with the Sun

3. The Sun belongs to a spiral galaxy like this.

4. A collection of distant galaxies spotted by the Hubble Space Telescope

These pictures show, from top to bottom, how the Sun fits into the Universe.

Our galaxy, the Milky Way, is a spiral galaxy, with the stars on arms that curve out from the center. It is so large that a beam of light would take 100,000 years to travel from one side to the other. Astronomers say it measures 100,000 light-years across.

But soon astronomers began spying other star systems in space. And they realized that our galaxy was only one of many galaxies in space. All these galaxies made up the Universe.

Astronomers estimate that there are more than 15 billion galaxies in the Universe. These galaxies are very far away from our galaxy and from one another. Between them is only empty space. So the Sun is one of many billions of stars in a galaxy, which is one of billions of galaxies that make up the Universe.

THE SUN IN OUR GALAXY

Our galaxy is called the Milky Way. It contains about 100 billion stars. The stars are clustered together into a flat disk, somewhat like a Frisbee. There is a bulge of stars in the center. The stars in the flat part make up arms that curve out from the bulge. The Sun is found on one of these arms, quite a long way from the Milky Way's center.

The whole Milky Way is turning around in space. From a distance it would look somewhat like a spinning firecracker. The Sun takes about 225 million years to make one trip around the center of the Milky Way. This period of time is called a cosmic year.

Light-Years Away

The distances between the Sun and the stars and the galaxies are vast. They are impossible to imagine. For example, the nearest star to the Sun is called Proxima Centauri. It lies more than 25 trillion miles (40 trillion km) away. And this is only a short step in space!

The "light-year," or the distance light travels in a year, is a very handy unit for measuring distances in space. Proxima Centauri is so far away that its light takes over 4 years to reach us. We can say that it lies over 4 light-years away. The light from other stars even farther away can take thousands of years to reach us. In other words, they lie thousands of light-years away.

The brightest stars in this picture lie about 40 light-years away from Earth.

When the Sun Dies

In about 5 billion years, the Sun will start to die. First it will get bigger until it is giant sized. Then it will slowly shrink again until it is a dwarf star about the size of Earth.

An enormous red Sun towers in Earth's sky in about 5 billion years time. Millions of years earlier it ran out of hydrogen fuel and began to die. It has since become a star astronomers call a red giant. It will start to shrink in size, finally ending up as a body only the size of Earth.

Astronomers believe that the Sun is about 4.6 billion years old. Like all stars, it was born from a huge nebula, or cloud of gas and dust. The nebula gradually shrank into a ball of denser, or heavier, matter. The ball got hotter and hotter. Eventually, a nuclear "furnace" lit up inside the ball, which started to shine as the Sun.

The Sun has been shining steadily since then, staying as bright as it is today. But all the while, it has been burning up the hydrogen it uses as fuel. In about 5 billion years, all its hydrogen will be used up. Then the Sun will begin to die.

First, it will start using other fuels to produce its energy. But this will make it swell up. It will get bigger and bigger and redder and redder and turn into a huge body called a red giant. Many of the stars we see in the night sky are red giants.

The Sun might swell in size a hundred times or more until it is more than 90 million miles (145 million km) across. This means that it will then be bigger across than the orbit of the planet Mercury. So Mercury will disappear. The next planet out, Venus, will become scorching hot. Earth will get very hot too, and any life on it will perish.

FROM GIANT TO DWARF

In time, the giant Sun will use up all its fuel. Its nuclear furnace will go out. Then it will start to collapse. As it shrinks, it will puff off some of its gas from time to time. This will form a colorful cloud around it, which will gradually grow bigger.

The Sun, though, will continue to get smaller and whiter. In time, it will shrink into a body called a white dwarf. The white dwarf Sun will be about the same size as Earth. But it will be very much heavier. A tablespoonful of its matter might weigh as much as a thousand tons!

Gradually, the white dwarf Sun will cool down and fade. It will become dimmer and dimmer until it stops shining altogether. Then it will die, becoming an invisible black speck in the Universe.

Sun is born

The life and death of the Sun. It was born in a cloud of gas and dust. It will swell up when it starts to die, then shrink again. Finally it will fade away.

the Sun in A.D. 2,000

red giant

planetary nebula

white dwarf

Blowing Rings

Astronomers know of other stars that were once like the Sun but are now dying. They can see the nebulae that the stars have puffed off at the end of their lives. The most famous example is called the Ring nebula because it looks like a smoke ring. In the middle of the ring is the star that is dying. This kind of nebula is called a planetary nebula. In small telescopes, it appears round, like a planet.

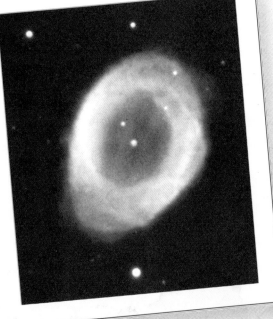

Exploring the Sun

Astronomers study the Sun in many ways. They use special telescopes at observatories on the ground. They also use satellites in orbit around Earth and probes that travel deep into space.

Because the Sun is so important to us, we need to know as much about it as possible. Changes that take place on and in the Sun can affect Earth. For example, solar flares can cause electric storms here. Changes in the Sun's heat output can cause changes in our climate.

Astronomers build special telescopes to study the Sun. Solar telescopes take the form of tall towers. They have mirrors on top to reflect sunlight down to an observation room at the bottom. In this room, astronomers study images of the Sun's surface.

Kitt Peak Observatory in Arizona has the biggest solar telescope in the world. It is called the McMath Solar Telescope. It produces an image of the Sun's surface more than 3 feet (1 m) across.

The tower of the telescope stands about 11 stories high. Its mirror reflects sunlight down a sloping tunnel cut into the mountainside. A second mirror at the bottom reflects the light to a third mirror at ground level. This mirror reflects an image of the Sun into the observing room.

This tall tower is one of the solar telescopes at the Mount Wilson Observatory, near Los Angeles. A mirror on top reflects an image of the Sun down the shaft in the center to the observing room.

The McMath Solar Telescope at Kitt Peak Observatory, near Tucson, Arizona. A mirror on top of the upright tower reflects sunlight down the sloping shaft and deep underground.

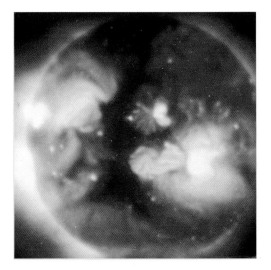

Above: The Sun as seen through *Skylab*'s X-ray telescope. The dark areas are holes in the Sun's outer atmosphere, or corona.

Right: Space station *Skylab* in orbit in 1973. It observed the Sun with eight solar telescopes, mounted in the circular dish you see in the center of the picture. The X-shaped panels carry solar cells to make electricity. On the right, you can see the patches astronauts used to repair *Skylab* after it had been damaged during launching.

OBSERVING FROM SPACE

Astronomers cannot get a complete picture of what the Sun is like using solar telescopes on Earth. This is because Earth's atmosphere blocks many of the invisible rays coming from the Sun. For example, it blocks X rays and many ultraviolet rays.

This is one reason astronomers send solar telescopes into space. In space they can study all the rays coming from the Sun. This gives them a much more complete picture of what the Sun is like.

Three teams of astronauts on the experimental U.S. space station *Skylab* carried out the first main study of the Sun from space in 1973 and 1974. They took tens of thousands of pictures of the Sun with ultraviolet light and X rays, as well as with ordinary light.

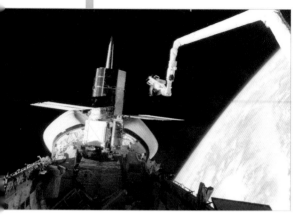

Above: Shuttle astronaut George Nelson inspects Solar Max after it has been captured and placed in the shuttle's payload bay in April 1984. After repair, it will be returned to orbit.

Above: The space probe *SOHO*, the solar and heliographic observatory. It was built by ESA (the European Space Agency) and launched by NASA.

Right: In July 1996, *SOHO* spotted a "sunquake" following a solar flare. It produced ripples that spread over the Sun's surface like ripples spreading over a pool of water.

OBSERVING SUNQUAKES

More recently, the Sun has been studied closely by the satellite Solar Max and the probes *Ulysses* and *SOHO*. Solar Max went into orbit around Earth in 1980, but it failed two years later. In 1984 astronauts from space shuttle *Challenger* mended the satellite. It then continued to work for several more years.

Ulysses was launched by space shuttle *Discovery* in 1990. This probe first looped around Jupiter before traveling to the Sun. It went into orbit around the Sun, circling over the North and South poles. It was the first time astronomers had been able to study these regions.

SOHO was launched in 1995 and traveled to a point in space some 930,000 million miles (1,500,000 km) from Earth. Its instruments study the Sun and its atmosphere in great detail. They keep track of the Sun's magnetism, temperature, and brightness. They also watch out for solar flares and "sunquakes," which are shock waves rippling across the Sun's surface. They have also spotted comets diving into the Sun.

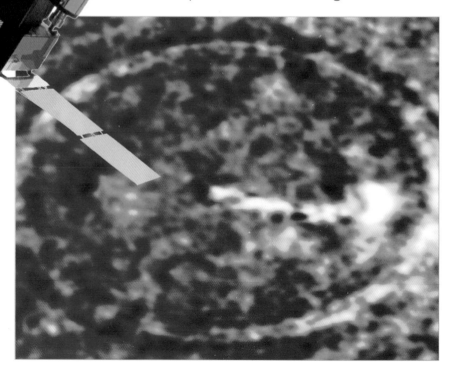

Glossary

aurora: colored lights that appear in the skies in the far northern and southern parts of the world

axis: an imaginary line passing through the center of Earth and the North and South Poles

chromosphere: the Sun's inner atmosphere

corona: the Sun's outer atmosphere

day: the time it takes Earth to spin around once on its axis

eclipse: what happens when one heavenly body moves in front of another and blocks its light

element: a basic building block of matter

flare: a powerful eruption in the Sun's atmosphere that gives out streams of particles

fusion, nuclear: the joining together of atomic particles, the process by which the Sun makes its energy

galaxy: a large group of stars in space

gravity: the attraction, or pull, that a heavenly body has on objects on or near it

light: rays from the Sun that we can see with our eyes

light-year: a unit astronomers use to measure distances in space. It is the distance light travels in a year, about 6 trillion miles (10 trillion km).

lunar: having to do with the Moon

nebula: a cloud of dust and gas in space

photosphere: the Sun's visible surface

photosynthesis: the process by which plants use sunlight to make their own food

planet: a large heavenly body that circles around the Sun in space

probe: a spacecraft that escapes from Earth to travel to a heavenly body

prominence: a great fountain of flaming gas rising through the Sun's atmosphere

red giant: a huge star that is dying

satellite: an object that circles in orbit around a larger body. Space satellites are spacecraft that orbit Earth.

seasons: regular changes in weather patterns during the year, brought about by the tilt of Earth's axis in space

solar: having to do with the Sun

solar system: the family of the Sun, including Earth and the other planets

solar wind: a stream of particles given off into space by the Sun

spectrum: a band of colors formed when light is split up into its different wavelengths

sunspot: a region on the Sun's surface that is darker and cooler than the rest of the surface

universe: space and everything in it—stars, planets, moons, gas, and dust

white dwarf: a tiny star near the end of its life

Index

JUL 2001